"Let's put the cupcakes in your basket," said
Little Red Riding Hood's mother.
"Mmmm!" said Little Red Riding Hood.
"They're for Granny – NOT for you," laughed
her mother.

Her mother watches her from the window.
"Now – off you go. And –"

2

"I know. I know – Don't speak to strangers in the woods," laughed Little Red Riding Hood.
"Mothers!"

Little Red Riding Hood ate her apple and
sang as she walked along.
But – oh! Who is this behind her?
A wolf is watching her from behind a tree.

"Good morning little girl, where are you going?"
"I'm going to see my Granny. She's sick in bed."

Oh, Little Red Riding Hood, remember – don't
speak to strangers.

"Goodbye," said the wolf. "Remember now – don't speak to strangers. Ha! Ha! Ha!"
The wolf ran off very quickly.
"Goodbye, Mr Wolf," said Little Red Riding Hood.

The wolf ran quickly
to Granny's house.
He went in.

"I am hungry," he said.
He opened his mouth wide and ate Granny in
one big gulp.
"Mmmmm!" he said.

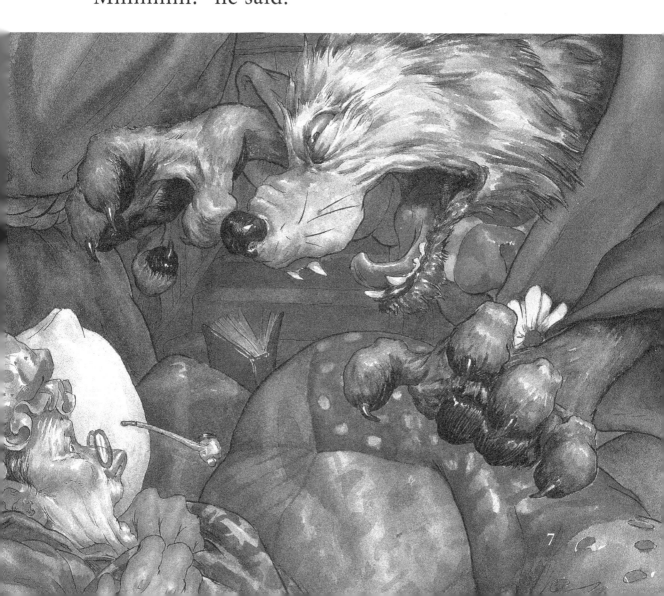

"Hello Granny! It's me, Little Red Riding Hood."

"Come in. Come in, little one," said the wolf, in Granny's clothes, from the bed. "You look pretty today."

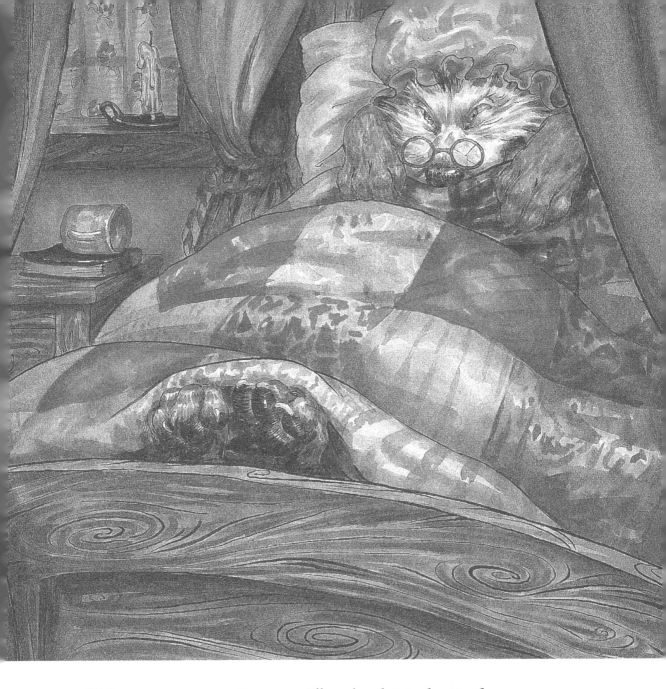

"How are you, Granny?" asked Little Red
Riding Hood.
"A little better. Thank you."
"Look Granny. I have some cupcakes for you."
"Thank you," said the wolf. "How nice!"

"Granny, why are your ears so big?"
"To hear you, little one."
"And, Granny, why are your eyes so big?"
"To see you, little one."
"And why are your arms so big?"

"To hug you, little one."
"But, Granny, why are your teeth so big?"
"To – EAT YOU, LITTLE ONE!"
And the wolf jumped from the bed.

"HELP! HELP!"

Little Red Riding Hood ran to the door.

"Mmmm! Dinner, dinner, here I come," laughed the wolf as he ran after her.

"Stop! Stop!" said a woodcutter.

He came in and stopped the wolf by cutting him with his ax.

"Goodbye wolf."

"Oh, thank you," said Little Red Riding Hood.
"But where's Granny?"

Granny jumped out of the wolf's stomach.
"Oh, Granny," said Little Red Riding Hood.
"Are you OK?"
"Yes, I'm OK," said Granny, "a little weak, but very hungry. Now where are those cupcakes?"

ACTIVITIES

BEFORE YOU READ

Look at the picture on the front of the book.

Make up your own story about a wolf and a little girl in the woods.

AFTER YOU READ

Look at the pictures.

1. At the start of the story, on which page is there a woodcutter?

2. Little Red Riding Hood carries cupcakes in her basket, but there is something else in there too. Can you find what it is?

3. Which of these things are NOT in the picture on page 14?
   goat, hat, wolf, bird, nightgown

Pearson Education Limited
Pearson
KAO Two
KAO Park
Harlow
Essex
CM17 9NA

and Associated Companies throughout the world.

ISBN 9781292240015

First published by Librairie du Liban Publishers, 1996
This adaptation first published by
Penguin Books 2000
11

Text copyright © Pearson Education Limited 2000
Illustrations © 1996 Librairie du Liban

Series Editor: Melanie Williams
Retold by Audrey McIlvain
Designed by Shireen Nathoo Design
Illustrated by John Lupton

Printed in Great Britain by Ashford Colour Press Ltd.
SWTC/01

The moral right of the author and illustrator have been asserted

Published by Pearson Education Limited

For a complete list of titles available in the Pearson Story Readers series please write
to your local Pearson Education office or contact:
Pearson, KAO Two, KAO Park, Harlow, Essex, CM17 9NA

Answers for the Activities in this book are published in the free Pearson English Story
Readers Factsheet on the website, www.pearsonenglishreaders.com